THE CONFESSIONS SERIES

Confessions of a Christian Woman

A Journey in Marriage

"A New Beginning"

Confessions of a Christian Woman

A Journey in Marriage

"A New Beginning"

Antonia Roman

Confessions of a Christian Woman
A Journey in Marriage
"A New Beginning"

Published by: Antonia Roman
Copyright © 2019 by Antonia Roman

All rights reserved. No part of this publication may be reproduced or transmitted in any form or by any means, graphic, electronic or mechanical, including photocopying, recording, taping or information storage and retrieval systems, without written permission from the author.

Scripture quotations marked (NIV) are taken from the Holy Bible, New International Version®, NIV®. Copyright © 1973, 1978, 1984, 2011 by Biblica, Inc.™ Used by permission of Zondervan. All rights reserved worldwide. www.zondervan.com The "NIV" and "New International Version" are trademarks registered in the United States Patent and Trademark Office by Biblica, Inc.™

ISBN: 9781070572888
Release Date: July 7, 2019

Library of Congress Control Number: 1-7012486501
Printed in the United States of America

Cover Photo: Floweramas Bridal Plaza

DEDICATION

I want to dedicate this book to my deceased mother, Andrea Carrion Roman. My mother was a very strong woman who always had a smile on her face. Her inspiration taught me to always see the best in people, love them unconditionally, and most of all, always give them respect. I will always remember the words that she spoke to me a long time ago *"Keep Reaching for the Stars."* And most of all; *"Do not depend on a man for anything, if you want something, get it yourself."*

I also dedicate this book to women who are struggling to find their voice in their marriage. You can find your voice with God's word (The Bible), salvation through Jesus Christ and the guidance of the Holy Spirit.

"For God so loved the world that he gave His one and only Son, that whoever believes in Him should not perish but have eternal life. For God did not send His son into the world to condemn the world, but to save the world through him."
(John 3:16-17, New International Version)

"If you love me, keep my commands. And I will ask the Father, and he will give you another advocate to help you, and be with you forever, the spirit of truth. The world cannot accept him, because it neither sees him nor knows him. But you know him, for he lives with you and will be in you."
(John 14:15-17, NIV)

TABLE OF CONTENTS

Foreword

Special Thanks

Back Story 17

Preface 18

While Still Single 24

The Journey Begins 32

The Transition 41

Getting Ready for the Fall 61

Losing Sleep 65

Pressing Forward 79

April Showers 95

Today's Reflection 115

Message to the Reader 118

Simple Prayer...123

About the Author...................................125

FOREWORD

Well, we all seem to be searching for something in our lives to satisfy a void that is missing. The only thing is that we don't know what to expect until we take that challenge head on.

I have realized that the way we accept the challenges in our given situations depends on the outcome. If we take the stumbling blocks of our lives and decide to fall or use them as stepping stones to become encouraged, it's really our freedom of will or choices we make that will make the difference. God will not force his will upon you or me in order for him to accomplish our destinies.

I've gone through many fast growing pains from a dysfunctional family and a quick first marriage that ended in a very sad divorce that should have driven me insane. Thank God that because there was someone always praying for me, it made a world of difference in my life, which was my mother.

Considering that I had my experience from my first failed marriage, I figured after nineteen years it's time to attempt once again not knowing what was ahead of me. So I did say, "I Do and I Will" and thought afterwards, "oh no what have I done?" Not realizing that I had some reservations from my previous marriage; I had allowed some discord. I was always so angry because it just wasn't working out! I felt lack of communication between my spouse and myself. We need to be very careful not to have such high expectations from someone when we should just allow the Holy Spirit to do his work.

I would like to take this time to first thank God, Jesus Christ my Lord and Savior, and the Holy Spirit for doing a mighty work in my wife, Antonia. For giving her the courage, wisdom, and revelation to write this first edition, CONFESSIONS OF A CHRISTIAN WOMAN, A JOURNEY IN MARRIAGE – "A NEW BEGINNING."

It has been a great encouragement to me personally and most of all spiritually. There's a lesson to be learned just as long as we are willing to hear the voice of the Lord!

THANK YOU VERY MUCH JESUS CHRIST FOR BLESSING ME WITH MY WIFE ANTONIA.

Your husband,

SC

SPECIAL THANKS

There are several people in my life who I owe thanks to mostly because of their support, love, and patience.

Pastors Ken and Karen Lightfoot; thank you for allowing me to spread my wings under your leadership.

To Kenia, Sylvia, Ismael (Beggie), Claudio (CJ), and Juan Ramon; my sisters and brothers who have always accepted me for who I am, also my father, Ismael.

I also want to thank my friends; Katherine Damigos and Judith M. Ruiz-Hubbard for being a listening ear.

Thank you and God Bless my husband, whose involvement in my life is the reason I write this book.

A special thank you to the financial contributors of the book:

        Anna Iverson
        Pastor Karen Lightfoot
        Marguerite Fair
        Judith M. Ruiz-Hubbard

BACK STORY

My dad left my mom when I was 7 years old, so I do not really have a memory of my mom and dad together as a married couple. I only recall my dad coming in and out of my life.

My mom passed away when I was 18 years old and it was not until about age 25 when I really started building a relationship with my father. I had to learn things about him that I really did not know, like what was his favorite color, food, music, etc.

With time I started to really get to know him and I fulfilled everything that my mother told me to do. My mother would always say to me that no matter what happened between my dad and her; I was to always love, respect, and build a relationship with my father. She never said anything negative about my father. And I wondered for many years how could she be so forgiving in her heart despite everything my father did to her.

I learned with time that you only get to understand things when you are in someone else's shoes.

"Listen, my son to your father's instruction and do not forsake your mother's teaching."
(Proverbs 1:8, NIV)

PREFACE

When I was growing up, I always said to myself that I wanted to be a single woman who would conquer the world by fulfilling my dreams. I wanted to enjoy life, be adventurous, and possibly travel. Although, I did not really travel much, my life so far has been full of ambition and special moments. I have always been a very outgoing person and I make friends wherever I go.

I like talking a lot and I am always asking people questions. I love being around people from other cultures. As a teenager, my friends were Italian, Portuguese, and Salvadoran. I found myself trying to learn how to speak their language. I was pretty good. I picked up on a couple of sentences. We all got along so well and always told each other that we would always be there for one another.

My friends were like minded like me, however, some of them started to pursue different things as they got older. They started to see life differently in their careers, and most of all in their relationships with their significant other. With time, it seemed like most of my friends were settling down, while I was still wanting to uphold being single. I just couldn't get myself into a serious commitment. I felt that marriage was a bad thing especially when I saw how my mom's life had turned out. My dad left my mom because she had a stroke and he did not know how to deal with it. What man does that? He leaves his wife because she got sick. That's one of the main vows you say when you get married; in sickness and in health. But then again, I don't know what my father was thinking at the time, so I don't know the answer to that. All I knew is that marriage was not for me. When people would ask me, *"When are you getting married?" "I would always say "never".*

The word never to my family and friends was shocking because when you are a Latina woman, who is Puerto Rican, ah, you are expected to get married, especially at an early age. But for me, that was not ideal. I did not want to do that, at all. My sisters both got married before the age of 21, and my oldest brothers got married in their twenties. So by the time I was in my mid twenties people were starting to wonder what was going on with me. I think my family just figured I was not ready. And they were right, for me, it was about me being single, no its or buts about it. I was just living my life. I had dated a couple of guys here and there who were nice. I was pre-engaged to a guy when I was 16 years old, but that only lasted a few months. It was my mom's idea; she felt since we liked each other there should be a formal commitment, so he bought me a ring. I thought it was cool. I was going around flaunting that little ring, and then eventually one day I found myself dating another guy at the same time.

Of course, I would take the ring off at times. I was young. I was not thinking about the repercussions. I was enjoying life. And then of course, the two guys saw each other; that was the end of both of them. Since then I learned that cheating was not a good thing to do. You end up hurting other people including yourself. It also disappointed my mother because she was with the hopes of seeing me walk down the aisle.

I decided instead it was just better for me to concentrate on working and nothing else. I was always working two or three jobs at a time. I was making money to support myself, and my bills. That became my norm. When guys would try to talk to me, I was always busy working, so I did not have to worry about being committed to anyone. I finally did meet a nice guy who I met at one of my jobs; he was special, until he started stalking me. He actually proposed to me but I was not in love with him, so I did not accept his proposal. My eldest sister said to me that I should have said yes. I told her, *"I don't love him."*, and she said to me, *"You could learn to love him."* I said to her, *"Are you out of your mind."* She felt that I had finally met a guy who could have given me a good life. I already felt I had a good life and besides the more he stalked me, the further distant I became, so eventually that ended too.

When dating comes to an end, it's not a bad thing when you are young because you feel like, oh well, I will eventually meet someone else, maybe. Either way, I just kept working as much as I could until I decided to go back to school and get my bachelors degree.

My graduation photo from Queens College in the year 2000

PREFACE

After, Graduation, about 9 months later, was when I met my husband. He was a guy I met in church. He was one of the musicians. He played guitar. He was nice to me. And eventually I found out he was a handyman. I hired him to do some repairs for me at my home. Like I said, he was a nice guy, he seemed to like me, and then one day he decided to ask me out. Right in the middle of one of the rooms he was going to repair, he comes out and says to me, *"I was wondering if you would go out with me."* I thought to myself, what? You are the handyman, and you want me to go out with me? Are you serious? Then he proceeded to tell me how he felt about me, and that he was hoping we could become an item. He said he had not dated someone in a long time.

Now, with that said. I did not know how to handle it because I had just came out of another relationship with a guy who dumped me. He dumped me so bad, that I cried for weeks. And now, I have another guy telling me he likes me. Geez, I was now saying to myself, don't do it. I think I smiled and giggled. And then eventually a few weeks later we started dating. It was casual dating and then it eventually lead to engagement and then marriage. I know what you are thinking. Never say Never. I get it. You are right. Sometimes we have to eat our own words. I did get married and my marriage took me on a journey I will never forget. As a matter of fact, I am still on the journey. Every day I wake up and thank God for his goodness and grace.

"For I know the plans I have for you declares the Lord, plans to prosper you and not harm you, plans to give you hope and a future. Then you will call on me and come and pray to me, and I will listen to you. You will seek me and find me when you seek me with all your heart." (Jeremiah 29:11-13, NIV)

WHILE STILL SINGLE

I was at a point in my life where I was fulfilling some of my dreams. I was in good shape, I had some money in my pocket, I had a mortgage on a home, and I was pursuing an Acting career while working in the Real Estate Industry. It was just a matter of time before I got a call to audition for what would have at least been a supporting role. I could have my dreams and as an addition to that be married as well.

Here I am on "The Brother" film set in New York

One day when my Fiancé; (now my husband) and I were talking he mentioned to me that he wished he could live near his mother. So, I took it upon myself to search for houses near where his mother lived. Before, I knew it I saw there was a house for sale. It was a house that was being auctioned off by the bank since the previous owners defaulted on their mortgage. I put the bid in, and was notified shortly after that I was the candidate to obtain the winning bid. I told my fiancé, (now my husband) that I had the opportunity to purchase a home near his mother. I think he was in shock when I told him. He said, *"Really?"*

So before I even agreed to sign the contract, we drove down to see it, primarily in the dark since the utilities had been turned off in the property. My fiancé (now my husband) asked me if I liked the house because he saw the expression on my face. I told him, I did. I notified my Lawyer; and next thing I knew I was the proud owner of two homes, one in New York and on in New Jersey. In my mind, I had already set up that I would just move from one house to another. It would be a no brainer, simple, quick and easy. Once I got done with the wedding, it would be smooth sailing.

I was still prepping for the wedding and time seemed to be going by very quickly. I remember I started to feel stressed because I had already picked all the dresses for the bridesmaids, all the tuxedos were rented for the groomsmen, the hall was all paid for, flowers, etc, you name it, but I still had not event looked at wedding dresses. I was taking care of everyone else except myself. Everything I was prepping for seemed to be a burden.

I was very tired. I started to ask myself if this was something I really wanted. From what friends of mine had told me, or articles I read in magazines, the bride starts to look for her dress first before doing anything else. Again, maybe I was delaying things because I really couldn't believe I was getting married. I remember one day I woke up and thought to myself, what if I changed my mind. What if I decided not to get married and just stay single, but then I looked at all the things I had laid out for the wedding, and the reality finally set in. It was time to look for a dress.

One day after work, I walked into a store that had some prom dresses. I asked the clerk if they had any wedding dresses. He told me to go to the back of the store and look at a rack that had some dresses on it. I walked back there and I said, *"Lord please let me find a dress my size that will fit me and will not cost too much money."* I went to this small rack and started looking at any dress that looked white. I stumbled upon a dress, I took it off the rack, and I was amazed. It was beautiful. It was a corset wedding dress that made your waistline slim and then it flared out with a train. I could not believe my eyes, it was exactly what I wanted. You see, on occasion I looked at wedding magazines and saw beautiful gowns that cost thousands of dollars. I knew I could not buy a dress for that amount of money, but somehow I felt God would supply the perfect dress and here I was in this store seeing the dress God had for me.

I immediately asked the clerk what size it was and he said *"Twelve."* I said, *"Twelve?" "I am a size three."* The clerk came over to me and said, *"The dress is a 12 model size, it should fit you."* So I waltz myself to the dressing room to try on this dress. It was a little difficult at first because I had never seen myself in a wedding dress, and I couldn't tie it in the back, so I just held it up the best I could. And I knew this was the dress. I asked the clerk *"How much is the dress?"* and he said, *"One Hundred Dollars."* I instantly smiled, and all of a sudden I felt happy. I kept looking at myself in the mirror. Now I could start to feel like I was going to make a major decision in my life and I needed to look my best. I knew it was time to take into consideration the countdown days to the wedding considering it was right around the corner.

    I started to ask God if I was doing the right thing. My fiancé (now my husband) had proposed to me during a church service in front of the whole congregation. I had spoken with some of the sisters in the church and they had advised me about what to prepare for in a marriage, somewhat. I had asked God one day on my knees in front of the altar if I was suppose to marry this man. God gave me a vision, I saw the back of me walking down an aisle and I was holding the hand of a little boy.

    At that time, I thought it meant I would have a child. Even though, that was another thing I always said; I was not having any children. Either way, I thought I had a confirmation, at least I thought I did. One of the sisters from the church asked me if I sought God's approval for this marriage. I told her yes, however, I never told her about my vision. I should have told her because I was still a young babe in Christ. Back then, I did not know what that vision really meant.

If I had shared the vision maybe she could have given me insight about what God was really revealing to me. Then maybe I would have made a different decision. But I said to myself, you know Antonia, you just have to keep going forward with what you planned out to do and make sure you have everything in place.

When my dad arrived a week before my wedding, I could tell he was happy that I was getting married, but I sensed he had a reservation. When he met my fiancé, (now my husband) for the first time, he gave me a look only a father gives his daughter. It was a look of concern. I assured my father in private that my fiancé, (now my husband) was a nice guy and that I knew what I was doing. My father looked at me and said to me, *"If only your mother was here."* I wondered if he said that because he thought maybe my mom would be able to confirm what he was sensing. My dad had been for many years asking me if I was dating someone; was I in a serious relationship; was I ever thinking of getting married. And here I was now finally fulfilling what he kept asking me, but for some reason it seemed like I was not meeting his expectations. Despite the fact that I may have in some way disappointed my father, he was kind enough to give the upmost respect to my fiancé, (now my husband) and even made sure to have a talk with him. It seemed like they got along.

The day before my wedding I came to the realization that I was really getting married. I know, you must be thinking, my gosh she has said this many times already in the few pages I have read. But you need to understand, I was the one who was making a drastic choice to go against everything I had always said I was not going to do. So for me, it was a conjuring thought process all the time in my mind. And it seems that twenty four hours before a bride gets married is when she becomes the most nervous and excited at the same time. I recall at the last minute I spoke with my dad and asked him if he had any money so I could at least get some last minute things for the wedding. I wanted to buy some additional wedding favors that I thought would look nice for the wedding. My father immediately gave me the money. I ended up feeling a sigh of relief because now I felt that everything was perfect. All I had to do now was worry about my heart.

> "God gave me a vision, I saw the back of me walking down the aisle and I was holding the hand of a little boy."

THE JOURNEY BEGINS

The next day when I woke up, the weather was good. July was a perfect time for a wedding. Some of the sisters from the church were helping me get ready. There was one sister in particular who was doing my hair and makeup. She made me look beautiful. I was a little nervous. I kept going over in my head, had I gotten everything done for the day to run smooth. As one sister was helping me close up the corset on my dress, she kept asking me *"Does it feel tight enough?"* I said, *"Yes, but make it a little tighter so it can be fully secured."*

Someone started to yell from downstairs that the horse and carriage were in the front of the house. I still remember how many people came out of their homes to look at the carriage. I know what you are thinking. Yes, if I was going to get married, I wanted to at least have like a Cinderella Wedding. Most people in Queens, New York don't see horse carriages unless they go to Manhattan for a tour ride. But today was going to be a day to remember especially in my neighborhood. I remember my dad helped me get on the carriage and as we started to go down the main roads people were waving at us. It was quite exciting. I was waving back to the people like I was Miss America. My dad was laughing. I started to laugh too. I could hear people in the streets saying in Spanish; *"Mira el novio y la novia." ("Look at the bride and the groom.")*. I was like, what? I'm the bride, this is my father. But no matter what people thought, I knew my Dad and I looked great. I felt for the first time like a Princess, I really did. I did not grow up having a lot of dolls or having a girlie childhood that was always playing dress up. I grew up poor, and I started working at a very young age, and had adult responsibilities. So for me, this was my fairytale moment and I really wanted to enjoy it.

My dad and I on my wedding day July 7, 2002

As we were getting nearer to the church, I could feel my heart starting to pound. A big nervousness came over me, and all I could do was smile. I remember getting off the carriage and walking towards the church. I started to walk up the concrete stairs and I could feel my legs becoming very heavy. Upon entering the church I felt even more nervous. When I got in front of the closed doors to the Sanctuary, my dad turned to me, put his hands on my shoulders and said to me in Spanish, *"Tu estas seguara que tu quieres hacer esto?" "Tu te puedes regesar.",* *("Are you sure you want to do this?" "You can turn back.")* My dad was looking straight into my eyes. I stared back at my dad. And for a split second I thought, you know, I could turn back. But what would people say about me. I would be perceived to be a quitter. I have never been a quitter. People would see me as a loser.

On the other hand, I could continue to enjoy my single life. But instead, I smiled at my dad and said, *"Ya yo page por todo."* *("I already paid for everything.")* My dad drew in closer to me and said, *"No importa, es solamente dinero."*(*"It doesn't matter, it's just money."*) And then all of a sudden the music started playing. I took a deep breath and said to my dad, *"Nos tenemos que ir."* *("We have to go.")* So my dad pulled away but I could tell he was a little disappointed and he said, "OK". I put my arm in his arm and I started walking down the aisle. When Antonia starts something she has to finish it.

As I was walking down the aisle, I was looking at all the guests. Some of my friends had looks of disbelief on their faces. My family members were crying, like really crying. It felt to me like I was walking in slow motion. I could see my fiancé, (now my husband) and everyone else down in front of the church. I was smiling and thinking, wow, Antonia, you are really going to do this. You are really going to change your entire life. You are really going to finally give away your freedom. Yes, I can do this, I have a plan; it's a good one. Because in my mind, I had already figured everything out. I was going to have a happy and healthy marriage. I was going to set everything up with my husband so that we could be a perfect couple. I was going to manage both houses and be debt free. I was already thinking that my husband and I would run a business. Man, I was even thinking we could do ministry together. I was going to prove to everyone that I was making the right decision. That I was going to be the best wife, because I was already the best fiancé, in my opinion. I had already handled everything. I had paid for this entire wedding myself. I have always been very independent and always had a plan. So this plan I followed through with today was going to go well because I had it all under control.

Then it seems like all of a sudden, the slow motion turned into a race; I was already in the front of the church altar and my dad had given me away. I remember looking at the Pastor and noticing how wrinkled his suit looked. His glasses were also a little crooked, and he seemed a bit nervous. I remember there was a distinct odor from his clothes. I did not really know this Pastor. He was not our Pastor. We were getting married at a different church because our Pastor from the church we were attending refused to marry us. Our Pastor told us that he could not marry us because he felt my fiancé, (now my husband) was marrying me in false pretense and that he was not going to take part in it. I was really confused, shocked, and couldn't believe what he was saying. When our Pastor told us this, my fiancé (now my husband) assured me that it was more of a personal issue with him than with me. So we decided to get married somewhere else. And here we are now, somewhere else getting married by a Pastor who did not even know us. I'm not saying this Pastor was not a nice fellow, but again, I knew nothing about him or him of us.

When the Pastor finally said, *"I pronounce you husband and wife."* I could hear people clapping, cheering, and some people still crying. As I started coming down the aisle one of my friends gave me a thumbs up. I smiled and kept walking. When we got outside, I felt like everything was going real fast; the reception, saying goodbye to everyone, getting back to the house, opening up all the gifts, and counting money to eventually go on a honeymoon.

It was now around two o'clock in the morning, and I remember sitting at the dining table with my husband and my father. I was so tired. I said to my dad, *"I need to undo this corset; I feel like I can't breathe."* So my dad and my husband started undoing the corset and they were both amazed on how tight it was on me, and the time it took to undo. As soon as the corset was undone, I felt my body expand and all of a sudden I became very sleepy. I remember saying to both of them, *"I am going to bed."* I went into my room, took off the dress and went to sleep on my daybed.

It was not until the next day that I realized that I did not have a wedding night with my husband. I got out of bed and went into the kitchen. My dad and my husband were sitting at the table. My dad looked at me with curiosity and he said to me; *"Te fuiste a dormir, descansaste?"* *("You went to sleep, did you rest?")* I answered him by saying, *"Si."* *("Yes")* A few days later my dad left to go back to Puerto Rico. My husband and I went on our honeymoon. It was on my honeymoon that I felt I had made the worst decision of my life.

The Poconos is considered a place for lovers. For me, it felt more like a place for misery. I remember when we first arrived we were given a nice accommodation because we were just married. As newlyweds you are given extra perks. The first day we were outside they gathered together all the people who just got married. The host said, *"We are going to play a game."* The game would entail finding clues to put together a puzzle to win prizes. I got really excited because I was like, wow, great; we get to play a game. For many years I was not really a game playing type of person. I felt for this occasion, I can let my hair down and have some fun.

The host explained the rules; he specifically said that when he would count to three all the men would have to run to a certain area to find clues. When three came, all the men started running. My husband just stood there; I looked at him and said, *"You have to go running.",* and his response was *"I don't want to play."* I was like, what, you're kidding me. So I took off running to catch up with the guys to find the clues. When I got to a tree where the clues were located, I saw it right away. But instead of picking it up, I told one of the men where to get it. And then we all ran back. When I arrived back my husband had this look on his face. Now the host says that it is time for the women to run, and my husband blurts out, *"I don't want her running!"* I was not able to play the game. My husband insisted on leaving that area and going somewhere else. I was disappointed. I told my husband we were there to have fun. He expressed to me he was not interested in that type of fun.

The rest of our honeymoon was very quiet. No games, no fun, just sleeping in the cabin, literally sleeping, eating, and then sleeping again. It was not what I expected it to be. I couldn't wait to get back home. I knew this summer was going to be a season like no other.

*"There is a time for everything, and a season for every activity under the heavens:
a time to be born and a time to die,
a time to plant and a time to uproot,
a time to kill and a time to heal,
a time to tear down and a time to build,
a time to weep and a time to laugh,
a time to mourn and a time to dance,
a time to scatter stones and a time to gather them,
a time to embrace and a time to refrain from embracing,
a time to search and a time to give up,
a time to keep and a time to throw away,
a time to tear and a time to mend,
a time to be silent and a time to speak,
a time to love and a time to hate,
a time for war and a time for peace.*
(Ecclesiastes3:1-8, NIV)

THE TRANSITION

When we got back home, it hit me that someone else was going to live with me. I was use to living by myself. The only time I ever had roommates was when I was 21 years old but that only lasted for a year. When you are so use to being independent, it's hard because all of a sudden it feels like you need to share space, time and things with someone else. You are so use to your own routine, that now you have to adjust your routine and have consideration for someone else.

It takes time to adjust to changes. That is how I felt, like things were changing. So in the beginning, it felt weird. I had to now get use to sharing the bathroom with someone. I had a certain way of doing things; my husband had a different way of doing things. I felt my space was being intruded upon. I know that sounds crazy. But this is how I felt, dude, you are invading my space. I really had to talk to myself and remind myself that I was married and had to consider the fact that this person was going to be living with me until death do us part.

THE TRANSITION

Things started to move quickly again. We visited the house in New Jersey which I had purchased six months prior to our wedding. As we were prepping some things, my husband's mom along with some friends of hers happen to swing by and brought us an antique bed set they were going to dispose of. We gladly accepted it because I still had my daybed and it did not even cross my mind that I needed to change the sleeping arrangements. It was a nice bedroom set, so we put in the master bedroom. Now, we had a matrimonial bed. It was a full size bed, a little small but doable.

When we went back home to New York, I had started to think about how we were going to do the transition from New York to New Jersey. I knew this big house I was living in, I would have to pack up. So I started packing and as I was packing, I was thinking about all the years I had been at this home. The many times my family and friends visited me. The many parties I had in celebration of many occasions. I was really going to miss this home.

I bought this home when I was 29 years old, and here I was at 37 years old getting ready to move. There was a part of me that was sad to leave it behind but I knew I was starting a new chapter in my life as a married woman and all I could think about was getting things in order. I knew I would be leaving all my friends and family behind, but I am really good in making friends wherever I go. So within a few weeks, I got a few friends of mine to help us with the move to New Jersey.

New Jersey House

When we finally moved into the New Jersey house, I came to realize that the house I had purchased needed a substantial amount of repairs. Our house was a nice size, almost an acre, and it had a really big backyard with big trees and a lot of overgrown bushes. Every window had an awning on it, so not too much sunlight came in through the windows. It gave the house a lot of shade.

The house was in good shape, but outside on the walls of the foundation, there were these two big holes where the concrete plaster had fallen. It was obvious that someone tried to fix it before but the repair did not last. I knew that eventually we would have to fix it. We did not have a refrigerator. The sink was pretty bad and cooking on that stove was out of the question. So we stayed at my mother-in-law's apartment for about a month.

My mother-in-law was such a sweet woman. She really loved on me in a way that made me feel like she was my mom. She was the only one on my husband's side of the family who came to our wedding. She had a cheerful and positive personality. My mother-in-law loved on everyone unconditionally and she always had a smile on her face. She was also a great cook. She was a good listener and would at times give me good advice. I remember the first time my husband took me to meet his mother, she was so happy. I guess it's because she knew that her son had not dated anyone in a long time, and here I was, a new girlfriend. I recall my husband saying to her, *"Isn't she so adorable ma?"* and his mom saying *"She sure is.*

THE TRANSITION

Once we finally moved into the house, I started to put things in place as I saw fit. I was trying to make the house look as nice as possible. Although, I did not have much money left in my bank account, I still bought things here and there. When I initially bought the house, I had left my fiancé (Now my husband) at the house for about two weeks so he could paint, do the floors and prep the house for the move. I think he was overwhelmed because the only thing he ended up doing was removing all the rugs in the house. So by the time we moved in, I had to deal with the disarray condition of the house. I was trying to get everything ready because I had to start my new job in New Jersey.

I started working at a Real Estate Office and for some reason I really thought I would be able to work both the New York and the New Jersey Real Estate Markets. It seemed simple in my mind but the reality was that the commute from South New Jersey to New York took two hours. In addition the tolls were expensive. So eventually, I did not go to New York as often as I had planned. Instead, I decided it was just time for me to get acclimated to my new surroundings.

I know that when you move to a new place, it takes time to get to know people. I have always been the type of person to talk to people. Everywhere I went I was introducing myself to someone. After all, I was seeing about acquiring clients, so I had to hustle. When you are from New York, you hustle, in a good way. I was really missing my home back in New York but I knew that I had to embrace a new community and make the best of it.

For my husband, it was not as easy for him to meet people. He was an introvert. He preferred to stay home and he did not go out much. Within a matter of weeks, he was very irritable and started acting a certain way towards me.

He started cursing and yelling at me. My presence seemed to bother him. Things were not good with my husband and I, and the irony is that people kept saying to me when they found out I was recently married, *"Oh, you are still on your honeymoon."* I didn't think so. I just smiled. In just a few weeks everything I thought about with my plans were not turning out that way. My husband was always in a bad mood. And I was always getting to hear about everything he hated or didn't like about me. It got to the point where verbal abuse started to take place. I was really overwhelmed by his horrible words every day. But no matter what, I woke up and put on the happy face. I started to see early signs of abuse I think when I was engaged but I just brushed it off. I convinced myself that it had not really happened, and that maybe my husband was just having a bad day that day.

----------------------FLASHBACK-------------------

[It was when we just came back from eating at a restaurant. We were in my Fiancé's (now my husband) car outside in front of my home. We were only a few weeks engaged and he was telling me that when someone is going to get married that they need to give up certain things. In my mind, I did not want to give up anything. I wanted to have everything I had plus be married. My Fiancé (now my husband) was explaining to me that I would have to give up being involved in so many things. He said, *"A woman should think more about doing things around the house and taking care of her husband."* I said, *"I'm going to take care of things but I am also going to do my own things."* I guess I came across a bit sarcastic, and I sort of stepped out of the car while still talking to him. He got angry with my response and he ended up pushing me away from his car. He said to me, *"You are not marriage material",* and he drove away. I said, *"Who does this guy think he is pushing me"*, but I just started walking to my house. That night I was like, who does he think he is telling me I'm not marriage material. Then I started to think about all the bad relationships I had in the past and asked God to make me marriage material. I remember saying, *"Hey, I am marriage material, I got potential, yeah."* The next day I called my fiancé (now my husband) and I apologized to him. I told him I wanted to be considered to be good marriage material and that I was going to try to better understand what he was trying to explain to me.]

-----------------END OF FLASHBACK--------------

Every time my husband would yell, I would always get very nervous which lead me to start eating a lot. I found myself eating to suppress the bad energy that was being forced on me. I woke up one day and had a hard time putting on my pants; they seem to be a little tight. I realized I had gained some weight. I noticed also that my face was a little swollen. I was going through some stress. Not only did I change my whole lifestyle, but

I left all my family and friends who I so much loved back in New York.

New York is a vibrant place, full of life, the city that never sleeps. On top of that, I was not doing any auditions for acting because now we lived so far away from New York. There were no trains where we lived and to get to the New Jersey Transit you still had to drive for about twenty minutes to get there before hopping on the train. It was totally different, it now would cost about a total of forty dollars to get to New York when before I could get around in the subway for about two dollars, another thing I did not anticipate.

As things seemed to pile up, I became a little anxious. It got to the point that when I prayed to God about my situation, I felt as though I had disappointed God and he was not hearing me. So one day I decided to start writing down my feelings.

AUGUST 1, 2002

Dear Diary,

I was debating whether or not to start writing down my thoughts as a new married woman. But today, I have no choice but to express myself. I have been married now for 3 1/2 weeks, and it seems that my married life compared to my single life has not changed. I found myself today, really trying to encourage myself. Work is slow, we have no funds to pay bills, however I still try to have the peace of the Lord. I came home and my husband gets angry with me because I did not get to cooking right away. He said, "Get out of my face". I wanted to cook, but obviously I didn't do it fast enough. I knew when I got married things would not be easy, but I keep telling myself, God fill me with your love, so that I could love my husband. Love is so hurtful. I hang on to the Lord, that's all I can do. Every day I seek something different, something new, but not quite just yet. Someone asked me today about my marriage. They said I looked happy. I told them, it's my patience and the Love of the Lord that sustains me.

Antonia

THE TRANSITION

I never thought I would start to do a Diary at my age, but I guess diaries are for all ages. My Diary was the only person I felt I could talk to besides God.

I prayed every day and I always cried out to God to take away this pain I was dealing with every day. The verbal abuse was every day. I even asked God several times, *"Why is this happening?" "Where did I go wrong?"* I should have listened to what everyone else told me. But it was too late. I made my bed so I have to sleep in it. I had to fix the mistake. But it seemed that no matter what I did, things did not get better.

This was one of my worst summers. August is one of the hottest months of the year, and we only had one air conditioner in the wall. We eventually got another air conditioner for the bedroom. I remember when we went to sleep that I was always cold and my husband was always hot. But when we woke up, I was always trying to be warm and my husband was always being very cold. How ironic. I was trying to make peace out of the situation. I just smiled and pretended like everything was alright. I got a call one day from my dad and he asked me *"Como va todo?" ("How are things going.")* I had to pause for a minute before I gave him an answer. I didn't want my dad to know what was going on so I told him everything was great. And then I changed the subject and asked him about Puerto Rico. I think my dad knew I was hiding something because I was doing too many pauses to all the questions he was asking me.

    I hid what was going on inside my household. My husband and I went to a local church and we would go to services on Sundays. I was always praying to God for help. On the outside everyone saw this happy couple but on the inside I was not happy at all. The minute we left the church there would be some type of argument or discussion that always made me feel like I did not even attend church that day. I felt every time God was giving me a boost in church, it eventually was being sucked out of me by my husband when we got home.

    At home, there were some days that were good and more days that were bad. And with every bad day I seem to indulge in food even when I was not hungry. I felt like I was becoming a blimp. In such a short amount of time I was gaining a lot of weight. I really couldn't believe it. I knew I was falling into a depression and food was my refuge. I also found myself constantly cleaning the house. I felt that if I cleaned the house a lot, it would somehow cover up the filth that was coming out of my husband's mouth. I was always nervous so I had to always keep myself busy. I started to go into the office more often just to get away from the insults.

My Co-workers at the office started to notice that I went from this delightful woman who was always happy to this quiet dreary woman who started to show signs of being unhappy. I recall one day I came into the office really upset and I started to cry because I could not contain myself, and one of my co-workers asked if she could pray for me. I accepted the prayer because I needed it.

If there was a time in my life when I really needed my mom was now. I wish she were alive so that I could find out if my dad ever did this to her. But I knew he probably didn't because he treated my stepmother really good. My stepmother is a nice woman as well. When I first met her in Puerto Rico she was always kind to me and she treated me with the upmost respect. It was with my Dad and stepmom that I saw a couple in what seemed to be a healthy marriage. I was very happy for my dad. He deserved to have another woman in his life. He had met my stepmom at a later age and he had become more mature.

My dad knew the mistakes he made with my mother and he had learned his lesson. I remember one day when he was visiting me in New York, he asked me for forgiveness for leaving me when I was little. He said that he was young and that when my mother got her stroke, he just did not know how to deal with it. He was in his early twenties; he was ten years younger than my mother. My dad also made it clear to me that he really loved my mother. I knew he did love her because he attended her funeral and he asked me if I could do him a favor.

He asked me if he could put a picture of him and my mother in the casket. He went into his shirt pocket, took out a picture and he gave it to me. I looked at it and this was the first time I was seeing a picture of my mom and dad together. It was a black and white picture and they both looked like such a happy couple. I took the picture and put it inside of my mother's blouse right next to her heart. It was obvious to me at that moment that they had a genuine love for each other but circumstances drew them away from each other.

So not having my mom and not being able to get advice from her, I took the time one day to visit my mother-in-law.

I told my mother-in-law what was happening to me. She was not surprised. She started to share with me some things about my husband I was not aware of. I knew of his prior divorce and two grown children; but what I did not know was all the suffering he had been through in his life. And on top of that, the upbringing that was not so good. I listened with amazement everything his mother was telling me. I couldn't believe that of all his family members, not one of them opened their mouth to tell me. That's when I figured out that I had married someone who had a lot of baggage.

Listen, I am not saying that I am perfect, but I only came into this marriage with a cosmetic bag. I had issues growing up, but considered myself to be very blessed in comparison with what my husband had gone through. I knew that things were not going to change unless my husband could get closure from some of those past hurts. We all go through things in life that get a hold of us. I have always been the type of person who forgives and moves on with any situation or circumstance I've had to face. I guess I am a lot like my mom. Seriously, someone would say something or do something bad to me, and if they came up to me to have a conversation, I would still talk to them.

That's how I am. I understand it does not work that way for everyone. There are some people who need time to get over hurts. However, the things his mother was telling me were things from like a long time ago. And I was saying, *"Really?" "And this is still bothering him?" "He hasn't gotten over it?" "Wow, that's crazy."*

When I left my mother-in-law's apartment and I was driving back home; I said to myself, ok we need to talk about this and get him to forget all this stuff from the past. When I got home, I started a conversation with my husband about some things to try to get him to talk about his past. He was not happy with me bringing up anything from his past, so he became very defensive and told me to mind my own business. So that is exactly what I did. But still in the back of my mind, now I was thinking about what was really happening.

I immediately became judgmental of my husband and was like, man, I am not dealing with a full deck of cards. That is what I really thought. The reason I say this is because my husband had major mood swings. One minute he was all nice and then the next minute he was a raging bull. I even said to myself, this guy is bi-polar. I remember one day I asked my husband if by any chance he was bi-polar. The look on his face said it all. So I just said, *"Hey, just wondering because of what's been happening lately."* I then walked away to avoid confrontation.

That evening I found myself crying with frustration because I didn't know how I was going to handle the situation. I felt like I no longer had control. I was always by myself in a good healthy environment. Now, I was in an environment that was toxic. It really was affecting me emotionally, and at the same time had my nerves shot. My husband had not found a job yet and I think that may have been part of his outbursts as well. Even though, he was doing some things around the house, it seemed to me like he was taking forever. I needed to financially get back on track.

I finally took it upon myself to get a second job. Now, that I was gone all day, it felt good. Because the more I was away from the house, the less subjected I was to what was happening there. I was always with the hopes when I got home at night that he would be sleeping. It was when he was sleeping that I felt things were peaceful.I would come home tired and I was always greeted by my dog. Sassy was the dog I already had with me when I met my husband. She was the one who was home all day with my husband. If she could talk the human language, she would have so much to say. On many occasions, my husband would yell and hit Sassy and I would go to her defense by picking her up and having her next to me. I could tell her nerves were shot too because she would start to pee around the house which is something she never really did. Animals can sense things as well. They can sense human feelings, whether it is good or bad. I loved my Sassy so much. I would always pray over my dog so that she would be protected by God.

  I felt like the more I prayed that I was not getting any answers from God. See the problem was that I was praying things like, *"Oh God, can he just shut up." "Please, I just need him to find a job so he can get out of the house." "I need him to change his ways."* These were prayers that at the time I thought made sense. This is how I was approaching things; I was telling God what I felt should be the way God should be doing things. I would say, *"When are you going to change him?"* It felt like a change was never coming, and I wanted to see it done like real fast. And when I did not see any results, I went straight to my Diary.

"I prayed every day and I always cried out to God to take away this pain I was dealing with every day."

August 14, 2002

Dear Diary,

Today is a day full of wasted energy. I find myself very depressed. I realize that sometimes we end up with some things we really don't want. I have doubts and concerns about my marriage. I am trying to work things out, but I'm so tired. It seems that no matter what I do, I can't get myself to loosen up to my husband. I don't have any desires to be intimately involved with him. Could it be that I confuse love for man as brotherly love? I am so turned off. I can't get any motivation out of me. I think it has to do with my circumstance. Financially, we are still behind. I sense a huge disappointment my way. I have already been affected and tears just keep flowing. My husband, is I guess comfortable with life. He doesn't seem motivated to do much. I can only work so hard to accomplish nothing. But, no matter what, I still have to stay focused on Jesus Christ. Every day I run the race but seem to stumble and fall. What is going on? I'm out of love. Lord, I ask, fill me up. Things are turning out differently than I had planned. I think I settled for less. I know I deserve better.

Antonia

GETTING READY FOR THE FALL

One day my husband and I got into a heated conversation. He came out and told me that in the Bible it clearly says a woman is suppose to submit to her husband. He said, *"Something you are not doing."* He went on to say how I was disrespecting him and I was not honoring him. My immediate thought was, excuse me, I am not the one going around here cursing up a storm or yelling at the top of my lungs. I have been doing everything for both of us. Who do you think you are? I can't submit to someone who is not nice or kind, that's out of the question. The more he drilled me about not being a good wife, the more it was getting in my skin. It got to the point where the more he complained about it to me, the more I started to feel as though as I was the one at fault. See what happens when someone knows how to manipulate someone else. The blame gets put on someone else for the actions they are doing.

My husband would say that the reason he was acting the way he was acting was because it was my fault. I was the one to blame for his actions. I was the inconsiderate one. He said, I was never home, I always out and about. And most of all, that I was taking him for granted and not taking care of home. Now, that one really got into my bones. How dare he tell me about taking someone for granted; if it wasn't for me we would not even have a house. I really couldn't believe what I was hearing. What an insult! I really couldn't believe what he was saying because in his head he had this whole thing all twisted. Now, I know he was missing a couple of screws. All I said to myself was; this guy really has issues. Issues that are problematic and those problematic issues are my problem too. When I was single I did not have the problems I was having in the little time I had been married.

I recently had a conversation with a woman who said to me *"Your first year in marriage should be wonderful."* I said, *"Really?" "Because in my marriage, I feel like I am at the end of my rope."* She laughed. I did not laugh because I knew what I was talking about. This, exactly what is happening now. I did not sign up for this. What was I thinking! How dumb of me to have fallen into this trap! I felt like a mouse that was caught in a trap and couldn't get loose. I found myself suppressing my feelings which only lead me to put more food in my mouth. The more I ate the bigger I was becoming.

One day a co-worker came to work with a pile of clothes that she no longer could fit into and she told us to look through it. I did, and found some really nice pieces, but the problem was that I saw that the tags were size ten and twelve. I was like, I'm not these sizes. But for some reason, I still ended up taking them home with me.

When I got home and tried them all on, they fit perfectly. I was looking at myself in the mirror thinking; wow, I'm really this size now. At least I felt good, to have some nice clothes to wear and not feel like I still had to squeeze into things. On top of that, I was feeling really down about myself, I knew I was depressed and I had let myself go a little. It's one thing to feel horrible in the inside but you don't necessarily have to look it on the outside.

I was always trying to encourage myself in the Lord. I would always pray, and there were times when this peace would come over me. I had a true rest in the Lord. I felt like God was now hearing me. It felt good to know he had decided to be by my side again. The reality is that God never left my side. He was always there right next to me. I was the one who was always just focusing on the carnal side of things instead of seeing things in a spiritual way. I started to feel a little more at ease. I had a sigh of relief moment as I continued to move forward with trying to make sure my house was in order and that possibly things would start to feel normal.

The weather was starting to turn and leaves were falling off the trees. We were raking leaves for weeks, or should I say I was. I couldn't believe how many bags I had to fill. On occasion, I would look up at the trees and say, *"I will eventually cut you down."*

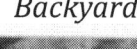
Backyard

LOSING SLEEP

I decided it would be best to get a third job. Now, I was getting home around midnight almost every day. I was so tired but I was starting to make extra money. Things started to look like they were getting back on track until I did not receive the rent check from my tenant at my New York home. This came unexpected and became a pattern so before I knew it the bank was threatening to foreclose my home. I was overwhelmed. Things were not going according to my plans. How could this be happening? I should have gone with my prior plans.

I was going to have another family move into my New York home. It was going to be a Section 8 contract agreement, which would allow for me to get money every month. But I let my husband convince me to rent it to a friend of his instead. As much as I wanted to do things my way, I still gave in. I was saying to myself, you see, this is what you get Antonia for not sticking to your own plans. You have the right way of thinking clearly how things should be. I was really disappointed with myself. I had no one to blame but myself since I ultimately made the decision. What was done was done. Now, I had to come up with another plan to see how

I was going to resolve this issue.

Out of desperation, I went up to my husband and asked him if he was planning on getting a job. That was like asking him to jump off a bridge. He got upset with me asking such a question. That he would look into a job when he felt like it. I made some suggestions about maybe working at Home Depot or Lowes but he took it as an insult. I felt it was a perfect match since he was a handyman. It made sense to me. Apparently, my suggestions were useless. I was dealing with a guy who didn't want to work. That was the clear picture here. Then I thought to myself; why am I expecting this guy to do anything when it is obvious that I am the man of the house. And from now on, that is how I am going to be handling things. That's right, because I am the man of the house! I walked away knowing who I was.

Listen, I have always been independent. I have always been responsible since I was little. Why can't he be responsible too? At that moment, I got so upset. I said, ok, from now on I'm not even going to acknowledge this marriage. I started at times to pretend like I was single again. I no longer went around telling people I was married. I was ashamed to even mention it. I primarily kept quiet about it because some of my friends were always going to couple events with friends and would ask me if I wanted to come along with my husband. What? That was totally out of the question. No! Are you crazy? Bring my husband to a couple's event? Not happening. So instead I laid low in talking about being married. I decided that I was not going to say my married name at all.

    Besides, with all the weight I had gained I was always forcing my wedding band on my finger. Every time, I put that ring on, it made me feel like I had a brick on my hand. It really did. This ring that had a Cross on it and crushed diamonds on the side made my hand feel heavy. However, I felt I was obligated to wear it because of my commitment. I wondered what would happen if one day I decided not to wear the ring.

    My husband always wore his wedding band and acted as though everything was peachy king in our marriage. I guess that was because he always felt he was the king. All he really knew how to do at this point was spend time on that computer. He was really handling deals well when it came to ordering whatever he wanted on that computer. I got to the point that when he was on it, as long as he was pre-occupied with it, he would not bother or insult me. It would even allow me some rest to start a new day all over again.

As the days were passing by, the Holidays were around the corner. The enthusiasm was not there anymore. I had no Joy inside of me. I barely put the tree up. Celebrating the birth of Christ has always been one of my favorite Holidays. I was not in a cheery mood at all like I use to be. However, I had already told my older brother that my husband and I would go to his house for Christmas.

My brother always had a get together on Christmas Eve with the entire family. It was a time for everyone to enjoy themselves, laugh, make jokes and exchange gifts. That day I was somewhat quiet and all of my sudden my older brother says to me, *"You look like mom, your face, and everything, even your body."* My mom was a little chubby when she was alive. She was half paralyzed so she was always sitting down and could not physically do much. So, I think he said it because at this point I was already a size eighteen. All I could do was smile and stare at everyone having a great time.

The weight gain really took a toll on my body. My back was hurting me all the time. I was no longer that young, vibrant, sexy looking woman from five months ago. I was pressing through with my life but I was not happy. I had never been this big in my life.

My self esteem hit rock bottom. There were times when my husband would look at my body when I was getting dressed and say, *"You are getting fat".* Like if I didn't know that.

As New Years rolled in, I was wondering what God had in mind for us. My expectations were that things would eventually fall into place, that my husband would find a job, and I could eventually be able to get the help I needed around the house. I needed my husband to really start thinking about contributing financially into the household. I mean what man decides he does not want to help pay for the roof over his head. I asked God, why was I going through this, and when I felt God was away again, I turned to my friend.

January 7, 2003

Dear Diary,

I know it's been a while since I've expressed myself. Today, I find myself in a pain that goes from my ear up to my brain. I'm exhausted; working three jobs is very trying. But, I have to make ends meet. I'll eventually be able to have some time to myself in a couple of months. Again, I'm disappointed. No wonder I never liked expecting things from people. The kitchen is coming along, slowly. Hopefully tomorrow I'll have the refrigerator set up. I have found myself sleeping less. My dog Sassy is always up. I sometimes feel she expresses my frustration. She's very talkative. My husband, he's fine. His usual self. Progression? Not as I would like it to be. Day by day. Patience. I keep telling myself, I guess being happy is for rich folks. Christians suffer much. I keep asking myself if I wanted this, why is it so hard. Marriage is hard. I feel like the candle in the wind. Today is my six month anniversary. It feels like years. I'm tired. I keep asking God to keep me strong. Give a sign. All I can do is just look at myself in the mirror. Much is said. Much is seen. I never give up.

Antonia

LOSING SLEEP

Every year we are used to setting New Year Resolutions. All I wanted was a normal marriage. I wanted to have a husband that was a Prince and I wanted to be the Princess. I wanted the New Year to be full of good things, happiness, maybe even some loving. But, even on New Year's Eve all my husband did was sleep. For some reason he hated New Years, he preferred I guess, to sleep away whatever sorrows he had. I wanted to do exciting things but all I could do was watch it on the TV very quietly or see it on text as everyone started texting Happy New Year. The old year is gone. A new year is here but with the uncertainties.

I got another call one day from my dad and started telling him about my situation. He suggested that I get an annulment if I was not happy in my marriage. I told him that was not an option because I did not believe in divorce and that the time had already passed to do so. I explained to him that I wanted to stop the curse in my family with all these broken marriages and divorces. At least, that was something I felt I could do. Maybe stop the curse. Kill the curse. I did not want to be another statistic. Like, if I even knew what the statistic was at the time. I was just making excuses. I was always trying to solve the problem.

For some reason, I always helped people solve their problems. But then why couldn't I solve my own problems? Why did I have such a hard time getting my home in order? Getting my marriage on the right track? What was it about me that just couldn't get things in proper order? I started to ask myself if I was the one with the issue. Maybe I was the problem and not him. I asked myself, is this why his first marriage did not last? And why he really does not have a close relationship with his children? So many questions were going through my mind. I found myself so overwhelmed trying to figure out the answers. I couldn't come up with any answers.

All these questions and thoughts started to really overtake my mind. I had met his ex-wife one day when we went to visit his daughter in North Jersey. His ex-wife was very similar to me in that we both worked hard and wanted to make the best of life. The only difference was that she got rid of him a long time ago. I couldn't believe how similar we were in personality. And then I ended up finding out she was in the same industries of Real Estate and Film/TV. How coincidental was that, that he married me with the same attributes of her.

All in all after we left North Jersey, I was thinking, too much of a similarity to me. Great, just great, I kept saying to myself. When I got home, I couldn't wait to talk to my Diary about everything.

> *"As New Years rolled in, I was wondering what God had in mind for us."*

January 10, 2003

Dear Diary,

Once again I keep telling myself, I'm not dealing with a full deck of cards. No matter how hard I try, there is always a problem. When will I even have peace. Silence. Just shut up. I need a vacation. Away from everyone. Six months. What a bride. Where's the groom? I hold on to my vow. By a small string I hold on. It's not easy being a wife. They tell me how classy I am, how impossible to believe my choices. I have so many dreams about what my life would have been like. I guess when you fulfill someone else's dream, you lose your own dream. You wonder about it every day. Is there still a chance? I believe there is a great chance. Just not now. My only dream, I still sleep on. I hope to wake up one day to it's reality. My feet hurt. Too much work. That's the best thing for now. Stay busy, ignore the insults, attend to the wild cattle for now. Once they've eaten they no longer speak. Silence.

Antonia

A few days later, his daughter called us to ask if she could come live with us. His daughter just had a baby girl and needed a place to stay. She had a disagreement with her mother. I told her she could stay with us. We had two additional bedrooms. I told my husband that we had to prepare and make accommodations for his daughter and the baby.

Upon their arrival, the first few days were fine. But eventually Sam was going through his mood swings again so he was yelling a lot and cursing up a storm. I think the situation was too stressful for him. New born babies cry a lot and they require a lot of attention. I tried to help with the baby as much as I could.

One day his daughter approached me to ask me why her father was being this way towards me. And I told her that he had been this way for a while and he just had issues. It was obvious to her that I was really trying to keep the peace. I was always handling things with my husband gently, if you know what I mean. This was not easy for me. I was now fulfilling the role of a step-mom, and step-grandmother, let alone a wife and bread winner. There was now a family in this house, and I wanted things to be normal.

The reality was that I did not know what normal was in a family. As I mentioned earlier, I really did not have a traditional family upbringing. The only thing I could do was approach it the best way that made sense to me. Let's just go with the flow, see what happens, and most of all get to know each other. This would be a good opportunity for my husband to bond with his daughter, in my opinion. Here I was again thinking about what would be good for him. I realized that you can't force things on people, especially if they are not ready. It was just a matter of time when more stress was on my shoulders. I was trying to accomplish so much; the days went by so fast. Just as I would lay down my head to rest; it was time to get up.

My routine made me feel more like a maid. I would wake up, prepare breakfast and dinner, go to work, come home clean sometimes at midnight, go to sleep, wake up, and start all over again. I had no time for myself. And then my husband would complain about how I was not spending any time with him. How could I? I was too busy taking care of everything. I was playing house while taking care of three children. I was just going through the motions.

I had fallen out of love. Was I even in love? On the inside I was dying, but on the outside I had this facade. As long as people could see a perfect me on the outside they would never ask me any questions. I started putting up walls. I kept ignoring my husband as much as I could. When he would talk to me negatively, I would answer him back in my mind. There were times I would even curse in my mind. I was always saying; *"When is he going to shut up?" "Shut up already!" "I am sick and tired of your nonsense."* I even got to the point that I was like, *"Till death do us part, can he just die already."*

I would say, *"God just take him already, he's a Christian, take him."* And I continued to pray to God, but again, I was praying for all the wrong things. I could tell that God was not happy with my prayer because he never answered anything I asked for.

One day our next door neighbor asked us if we would consider learning about a business venture. Being the person that I am, I was like sure, what is it? They explained it was an online website where people could buy your products. We attended a seminar and saw a lot of people that were making great money and having a fantastic lifestyle. I recall my husband saying to me, *"What if we could be like that."* I signed us up to try the business but realized it took work to get it going. Now, how much more could I put on my plate? Maybe my husband could help me with leg work, research, etc. Unfortunately, he really was not interested, but I figured I would try it anyway.

I was always an ambitious person. Always reaching for the stars like my mother told me. But for some reason my current stars were falling stars. I felt like I could never get to the place I was intended to be in. Why was I in this place to begin with? Should I have even gotten married? There is a place in the bible that says it's ok to be single.

"For the unmarried and the widows I say that it is good for them to stay unmarried, as I do."
(1st Corinthians 7:8, NIV)

PRESSING FORWARD

At the Real Estate Office I had built relationships with several of my co-workers. They were very kind women who encouraged me when I was really down in the dumps. I admired some of those women because they had been in the industry for a long time. We were like family. It was a place away from home. As a matter of fact, I spent a lot of time there even when I was not working my lead shifts.

Business for me started to pick up and finally I was acquiring a client base. I was grateful to God that things looked like they were coming along. I felt that God was starting to answer some of my prayers. I prayed for deals; how else could I make money. One thing I thought about was where I would be in another ten years from now. How was my future going to look like? Just then, I had an encounter with a co-worker and I went home to write what happened down in my Diary.

September 16, 2003

Dear Diary,

Today while at the Real Estate Office, I realized that one of my co-workers (aged 80) was limping. She said how the doctor told her to take it easy. Her comment: "If I take it easy will you pay my bills?" I had said to her that I had heard she had another job besides real estate as a receptionist. She seemed bothered that I asked her that question. I assured her that I was just asking. Then it hit me. This 80 year old lady works 2 jobs, and does not have security. I then said to myself, I don't want to be like her. I don't want to be 80 years old without security. It rushed me home to listen to more tapes. I have to become Diamond, Go Diamond.

Antonia

I continued to pursue the side business with the hopes of gaining a high rank status. The more I wanted to do it, the more I wanted to gain that status. As time went by, I was trying to get more people to be part of the business, but was failing immensely at it. I was at the point where I was disappointed. Because in my mind, here I was again thinking that this new venture could help me get out of my situation, quick. I had to remind myself that what I saw in other people took them years to develop. For me, I did not have years, a needed a quick fix. It did not work out. I was too tired to even run that venture so I decided to cancel my membership. At first, our next door neighbors were a little disappointed, but then about a year later we found out that they left that business as well.

I have always been a go getter, trying new things, wanting to explore the possibilities. Even when I thought I could do something out of my comfort element, there was something in the way. I blame myself. There was no way realistically that I could take on another project to do when my plate was so full. All I could do was express myself by writing in my diary.

November 10, 2003

Dear Diary,

I'm tired, very tired. It just seems that no matter what I do or say it does not reflect on people. It's about 11pm and I just finished moping (mopping) the floor. It seems that if dust exists, it just exists and nobody does anything about it, but me. I feel like I get up cooking and go to sleep cooking. All my days are full of double jobs. I can't wait till I get my own "margarita". I will then feel released from any duties in my life. Christmas is around the corner, again another holiday feeling gloom. My marriage is not cheery at all. The responsibility of a wife, housemaid, stepmother, grandmother and bread winner and psychologist just seems overwhelming. When am I getting rest? Only when I sleep. If I knew what I should have known then, I still would be single. I miss being single. A lot. I just have to grin and bare it. I never knew I would get a full baggage of nothings. The only one who gets me anything is me. I feel that I have a grown child for a husband. He's always complaining, never happy, criticizing everyone, and expects everything to be done for him. Sometimes in life, people don't amount to anything because they didn't want to. I still have dreams I intend to fulfill.

and the only one who is going to fulfill them is me. Sometimes I just want to walk away from everything. I deserve better. I put myself in this circumstance. How do I get out? Till death do us part. That's right. No sooner. I guess it's a good thing I get a tax write-off. That's the benefit I guess. I miss New York. However, I really like where I'm at. New Jersey. It's good. Then again wherever I am, I survive. It's been a long time since I've had a real sweet kiss. I miss that too. Maybe soon; someday.

Antonia

The day finally came when my stepdaughter said she was going to be moving out. She explained to me that she could not continue to subject the baby to her father's behavior. I told her, I understood. *"It's one thing if I have to put up with his craziness, but you don't have to."* I felt horrible. She was right. I could not even have enough courage to confront my husband. I was too scared. I looked like a tough cookie on the outside, but I was a wimp on the inside. When she finally left, it didn't matter to my husband. He was ok with her leaving. The only thing I can say is that he was not sure why she left. I wanted to say to him; Because you are a Monster! You are a terrible husband and father! You disrespect people; you are nasty, and always negative! But, I could not get myself to say that. I was afraid of what would be the consequences. My husband never hit me, but he sure did punch some walls.

I remember one time he was so angry that he took a hammer and put a hole through the plywood in the basement. He said I made him do that. For some reason, I was apparently making my husband do a lot of things. My nerves were so shot that day; I ate a lot of sweets to try to calm my nerves.

For a split second I felt like a failure. Maybe I was the one causing all this trouble. I noticed that just my presence alone would make my husband get angry. What was it about me that triggered this? Is it because I didn't love him? Did he know that? I never told him. Or was it because he didn't love me? This is not love. How can you love someone and treat them this way. I had come to the conclusion that he did not love me and that what our Pastor back home said was true. Maybe this was false pretense. Did my husband marry me just to have a roof over his head?

I knew that the Covenant we made with God was sacred, so then why would he have done that? Why marry me and not just live with me? He had been divorced for fifteen years. Could it be he did not get over his previous marriage? There were questions I started to ask myself with the hopes to getting some answers. But every time I would try to bring up something about his past, he would share a story but not the one I really wanted to hear. I wanted to know the scoop on what was making him act this way towards me. I was trying to see if I could get to the root of the problem. Didn't he understand that if he would just let go of his past, things would get better.

My husband was sharing about abandonment, that he felt he was abandoned when he was little. Always felt abandoned. Then he brought up a story about kindergarten. It was something that happened to him at that time. I was listening, and finally I said, *"You are not little anyone."* *"Geez, you are a grown man."* Doesn't he know that he is at an age where that should not matter anymore. But as my husband continued to tell me the story, it was as if it just happened yesterday.

For him, since it was still fresh in his head, it did just happen yesterday. I knew I had my work cut out for me because I thought to myself, if I have to deal with this situation, there are probably decades of other stuff I have to deal with, but at least this was a start. It was better that he opened up to me with something, then with nothing. The question now was how can I help him?

As I mentioned earlier I was still a new babe in Christ, I did not know much about how to handle this situation. I felt that this was something in an area of another Christian male needing to step in and help. I knew that would not be possible since my husband did not want to even make friends, let alone tell other people his problems. I think I said a prayer and then walked away.

But it really had me thinking even more about my husband and his state of mind.

One day I got a call from my father that he wanted to bring my stepmom to visit us. I kind of swallowed my thoughts because I kind of felt like it was not a good idea, but instead I told him that was a great idea. I immediately informed my husband and told him that we needed to accommodate my father's visit. So we prepared for their arrival and got the guest room ready.

During my parents visit, one day on a Saturday, when Sam was not home, my Dad said he wanted to talk to me. As we were eating breakfast he said, in broken English *"I see that you really put this house together but what I don't understand is why you are never in it." "It's very obvious to me you are not happy."* Then I proceeded to tell my Dad that things were a little shaky with my marriage but that I was trying to make the best of everything. I even told him I was still trying to figure things out about how things should really be in a marriage.

My father started to tell me about his relationship with my stepmom and what they did for each other. He told me that they shared responsibilities, helped each other financially, and most of all did things together. I told my Dad that's good, that I was happy for them. However, because I did not have that opportunity to see an example of that when I was growing up, he couldn't blame me for not knowing how to do marriage. I also told him that if I could do it all over again, I would not have gotten married. But that I had made my bed and I had to lay on it. It was important for me to do my best. I caught myself and apologized to my Dad and my stepmom. I explained to them that I was so overwhelmed with some many things. They told me that they understood and would be there for me. I knew they meant it.

That night I was asking God again, why do I feel like such a failure? When will I see a breakthrough? How could I prove to my parents that this marriage was going to get better? How could I get my husband to be nice, happy, or even quiet? And when God was silent; I turned to my friend.

November 23, 2003

Dear Diary,

I came to realize tonight that my husband has a gambling problem. Ebay has really taken over his self control. A man that does not pay any bills, nor the roof over his head. He is quite content with life. Again, the baggage of nothings. I had a peaceful week and I understand that no matter how much you can try to influence a person, influence really comes from within. You must want to have it. To really have it. Self satisfaction is a mankind solution. Sometimes we satisfy ourselves with the things that are of no significance. Some people just exist, get a free drink and food, paid by others. While the rest of us slave everyday to have a plate of crumbs daily. It is no use of a woman who works harder than a man to hold a home together. Especially when the man exceeds every earning. Always. Those who never had anything seek nothing. Those who always had something struggle everyday to have a little something. Bills every day, lack of money. I try to make sense of it all. But it always boils down to the same solutions. Exact. No Change. How long will this continue? I wonder. When do I draw the line? It really wouldn't matter. When no one cares. No consideration. Especially when you are told they do it because they want to. At other people's expense. How can I succeed when I sleep with the opposition? Again, I feel a child next to me and not a man. What is a man? Someone who is gentle, enough to have a lady by his side, perfumed, pretty, well dressed and a blossoming flower. I find myself a scorned thorn of leftover rose bushes. Wiped out. Wondering if there will be a next season. I am trying to maintain the grass green. But the weeds are over powering. No breath. No sense of relaxation. A glimpse of sanity and then terror arrives. A new nightmare. Back to the old drawing board. I'm torn between my love, vow and commitment. I am not a quitter. Although walking away is so easy. But very hard, I am here on a mission. To be fulfilled? How Long? Only God knows.

Antonia

My parents visit made me feel happy. I was having a good time with them. I tried to take them wherever I could, and keep them away from the house as much as possible. That was the best way to avoid any confrontations. My dad knew what was up. He was not dumb. He could see that things were not good. He could see that I was being taken advantage of. So at times my Dad would say things that gave indirect attention to my husband. And of course, my husband would throw indirect statements back to my father. Despite the conversations back and forth, my dad always respected my husband. He never really got out of hand. But you could sense the cold in the air.

One day it started to snow, and my stepmom could not believe what she was seeing. She lived in Puerto Rico her whole life and she never saw snow. We went outside so she could feel the snow. It snowed a lot. She was really amazed. I heard her tell my dad how happy she was that he brought her on the trip. Wow, how sweet. I made sure to take pictures of them in the snow. We had a fun day.

My Dad and Stepmom after a snowfall

After the Holidays, my parents decided to go back home. I knew it was time to deal with the usual. My dad told me he would visit me again, so that left me with some type of assurance of something to look forward to despite everything I was going through. Again, I started to write down my thoughts.

January 16, 2004

Dear Diary,

I have really come to the conclusion that I am not happy in my marriage. It just seems that I continue to go through the motions, it really doesn't help. Today, I am frustrated. My husband is still his usual self. He hates the world, including himself. Not much has changed as far as our finances. He still does not want to work, I feel that it has gotten to the point where advantage has taken place. I am under the impression that life in general was meant to be easier And my marriage is the total opposite of that. Today, again tears flow because I continue to receive disappointments. I am truly a warrior at heart, battling everything on my own. The verbal abuse has gotten worse, not better. I just want to get away, fly away from it all. I need to get away for a while, take time out for myself. Live a little. Take time out and spend with Jesus. I know he will give me comfort. I tell myself it's going to be alright. I am the only one that can make a difference. The Joy comes from the Lord. But still, I am not happy. Not happy at all. I think my husband is not happy either. But his advantage is the roof over his head. No worries, no cares, no man. The child always beside me demanding, wanting to control. It's getting worse, not better. Sometimes I wish he would just disappear. Go down South, go wherever, just away from me. Get a life. Start over. No such luck. The ugly get uglier. Never mind. Who cares. I care. I really care. That's why I struggle so hard. Only I can make a change. I'm torn between a hard rock and a brick wall. I miss the real marriage love, affection, desire, excitement, it's not there. Never was, never will be with my husband. Not this guy. Maybe another guy. Maybe no guy. Maybe the single life all over again. Should have left well alone. Should have married John. He would have made me happy. He always went the extra mile. Where is my true love?

Antonia

APRIL SHOWERS

Spring was near and here I was again dealing with the lawn. I knew that I would finally get rid of all those weeds in the front and back yard. I really started pulling those bushes out, anything that I felt was dead I was making sure I took out. I was on a mission to revive the look of the outside of the house. But every time I would turn around to go into the house through the back door, there were those two big holes on the wall. I don't know what was taking so long for my husband to fix that. He always had an excuse, it's too cold, it's too hot, it's raining, etc. I just knew that we had to fix them because the bigger they got the more damage it did to the house. Water would pour in through the cinderblock affecting the foundation. I had to always clean up the mess in addition to the house already being dreary.

I really wanted sunshine to come into the house. Finally after much begging, my husband removed the awnings. It made such a difference. It made the house feel like it was somewhat alive. My husband did not like all that sunshine. He said it made the house feel hotter. That's what I wanted. I wanted some type of warmth in the house. I got so excited! I went out and bought a new set of pretty curtains.

I was determined to make the house look as nice as possible by really decorating it. It was almost like if something sparked in me. I don't know what it was. But it seemed to put a smile on my face. It almost felt like it was a sign of a new beginning. I saw also that my husband seemed a bit different. I asked myself, how long was this going to last?

Now many months had passed and the tenant in New York never paid the past due rents, so I started to pay the mortgage for the New York home out of the money I had for the New Jersey house. So it got to the point where now the bank in New Jersey was threatening to foreclose on the house. I found myself extremely overwhelmed, again. I hated the fact that I felt I was losing my grip, slipping, not being able to have things under my control. I was so upset. I felt there were times I just wanted to throw in the towel. I kept asking myself, how can this be happening? Why is this happening? I can't get a break!!!!!!!!!

Here I was losing everything I had ever worked hard for, and no one seemed to care. I started to question God, what is the Christian life all about? Why do I have to accept this? I want to kick myself in the head.

I was starting to really get angry, but I could not express it. I would look at myself in the mirror and in my mind I would say, *"Why aren't you being bold?" "Tell him to get his butt off that computer!" "Just tell him to pack his bags and get out!"* In my mind, I was yelling but nothing was coming out of my mouth.

I was too afraid, my nerves were shot. I felt like I was just a functioning mannequin. I went to work, church, events, and places like nothing wrong was happening in my life. As if I had it all together. But I didn't have it all together. I use to go to the altar at the church and say every time in my mind. *"GOD WHY AREN'T ANY CHANGES TAKING PLACE?"* And tears would just flow from my eyes, uncontrollably.

I was always praying. The praying is what kept me functioning on a daily basis. Even when my husband cursed at me, I prayed. Now, of course there were times when I wanted to curse him back. In my mind, I would be saying; *"SHUT UP!""SHUT UP ALREADY!" "I'M SICK AND TIRED OF YOUR WORDS!"* I would even say; *"DROP DEAD ALREADY!"* But then ask God for forgiveness because I knew that was not the right thing to think. And then I would pray for God's protection. It wasn't until one day I prayed and God revealed something to me. I was getting ready for work and I was by my jewelry chest, I was putting on my jewelry when I looked out the window. There was a tree right next to our side window and some of the branches were near our window. I noticed something moving on the branch. I saw a bird sitting on a nest. This bird was a little chubby. And then all of a sudden I saw another bird come flying down and it had some straw in the mouth. It laid down the straw next to the other bird and the nest. I saw the bird leave again and then bring more straw. As I watched the activity of these two birds, I realized that the one bird was a female who was pregnant. And the other bird must be the male and he was building his house for the new family they were going to have soon. As I looked on in amazement, I was reminded of the scripture: *"Look at the birds of the air, they do not sow or reap or store away in barns, and yet your heavenly father feeds them. Are you not much more valuable?"* (Matthew 6:26 NIV)

Upon being reminded of this, I felt a comfort come over me in knowing that my heavenly father has everything under control and that he will supply all my needs. Then a couple of days later I saw that the baby birds were born, and now the mother was feeding them. I looked forward to waking up to see the birds in action.

Then the good news came, my husband got a job. He was able to work at the same senior citizen building his mother lived in. I was so excited and pleased. Finally, I felt like things were moving along. Once he would get his paycheck he could start contributing to the bills. I still remember the first time he got paid. I was anxiously waiting for my husband to quickly come to me and say; Honey, here is some money; do you need more? Let me know. When that didn't happen, instead I ended up going to my husband and asking him if he was going to help with bills and the response he gave me, I never expected.

My husband proceeded to tell me that as long as I was making money there was no need for him to give me money for anything. That the money he was making was his money. I was shocked! I couldn't believe what I was hearing and I couldn't understand it. What did he mean by his money? Every dime I have earned I used for both of us. There was never in my mind my money, because had there been that thought in my mind I would be like excuse me, see you, take care, I'm moving on.

On the contrary, I always gave of everything that I had. As I was still hearing his explanation of why he was not giving me the money, I couldn't believe it! I couldn't believe his reasoning why he couldn't contribute to the household. So things stayed the same, they did not change at all.

Now that he was earning money, he was always spending it. The UPS truck was always at our house. My husband was ordering guitars, and every time a new package arrived, he would tell me how much he wanted something like that since he was young. All I could do was smile, but inside I was burning up. I think it got to the point that I did not want to even talk to him, so I gave him the silent treatment. When I felt I couldn't take it anymore and really needed to express myself, I turned to my diary and as well wrote a letter to my husband.

APRIL SHOWERS

June 11, 2004

Dear Diary,

Well it seems that as time goes along things change and they don't change. I'm waiting on the Lord. For his grace is sufficient. It seems I am about to loose my house. We are 4 months behind on our mortgage, and once again my husband refuses to sell any of his guitars. If he just sells 2 guitars we can resolve our past due payment. But he refuses. He said that he does not want to sell anything. I am trying so hard to see what I can do. Sometimes life is full of surprises. You sacrifice, but no one else does. Sacrifices are for winners, only I know I'll win some day. God is good, he will never forsake me. He gives me the peace. He sustains me. I have peace. So many things change, but some people never do. What can I possibly do to convince my husband that life is not about Ebay. Yes, he started a new job, but still his love for the Ebay is never ending. I don't know how long I can keep this up. Pretending. Wondering. Will the real man wake up. Or will he forever sleep. Sometimes, every time I feel like the man. I am the man. Yes, I am. Should have been born a man. But God made me a woman for my patience. Can God change him? Only he can. But people need to want changes. Changes, Changes, Changes, sounds more like chains. What a life. How much longer? Till death do us part. Bye for now.

Antonia

June 11, 2004

Dear Husband,

I am writing this letter because I think it is the best thing to do. I find myself lately very upset about everything that is taking place. I am trying my best to contain everything that is being said and done to me. I thank God that he is really sustaining me, and giving me comfort and peace. In reference to this house and it possibly going into foreclosure, I am totally taken back by the fact that I seem to be the only one concerned in it's fullness of the consequences we are facing. I want you to understand that we must resolve this by June 30, 2004. The entire past due amount plus the attorney's fee must be satisfied. By July, a Marshall will come here and give us a notice of the day and time we must be out of this house. If we are not out by then, they will bolt lock this home. Now, considering that the prior family that lived in this house went through the same thing; I don't see a reason why we need to go the same route. I really need to know how much do you really care about this home and our marriage. I believe that I have done much in God's eyes in working at our marriage and home. I sacrificed coming to New Jersey, and starting over a new life with you and our marriage. I have worked every day mostly about

2 years now. I never really complain. I try to comply with what is needed in this home. I don't consider myself a selfish person. I do what I have to do. I am really shocked that you would tell me for us to ask the church to take us in. The church is not responsible for us. We are responsible for each other as a body of the church in our own home. I know that it is hard for you to depart from your guitars. They mean alot to you. However, if choosing between your guitars, and our home is a difficult decision to make then I have really been blind all this time. I would expect as my husband in a situation like this you would sacrifice the little you do have because I was willing to do the same. If you find yourself confused about what your decision needs to be, and quick that decision must be, then you may not be certain about our relationship. You know every time you tell me that you can't stand me and that maybe I want out of this marriage (I see where the marriage is going in your words). Maybe you don't want to be in this marriage. I know that God changed my way of thinking when I decided to marry you. And I have stuck through no matter what. I need to make something very clear to you. If we have to sell this house, I really do not see us staying together as a couple. I will have no choice but to stay with a girlfriend in a room. Because I will be so devastated that I would want to be left alone for a while. I

have stuck by you no matter what. But this to me would be like a slap in the face. I'm really hoping that God can work in my heart to sustain me from thinking the worse of you. Because I know that you are a product of God that is unfinished and God has already shown me the finished product. I wish you could see what God has shown me. Husband, you are a gift to me from God, I have tried to take care of this gift no matter what. (That is aside from not being sexually involved with you.) I need to always make sure you also have a roof over your head. I found myself asking people if they could have a spare room for a guy (my husband). I'm still thinking about you no matter what. This should not be to this point. Our marriage has to be based on sickness, hard times, financials, you name it. I'm here Husband, I will always be here. I am so sure that God is blessing both of us with your new job and my upcoming new job. He has allowed these things to take place. Do what is right for us. I hope you do not take this letter offensively. The letter comes with Love. I really need you to take care of me, the way you are suppose to love the church. If you love what's right, you will do what's right. Tonight, I really would like for us to talk about this. I am no longer going to hold in my thoughts or feelings. I am definitely going to start letting you know how I feel because I have realized that the only way this is going to get better is by telling you what I want and expect you to do as a man, and my husband, and my brother in Christ. I'm sure you feel the same about me in return. I think it is time to lay things on the table and get over the fact that life is serious and life comes only from God. We cannot take for granted our every day breath and what he has given us. I believe God is doing something new in my heart. And he wants me to express it to you. I love you Husband. I know you say you love me, but action speaks louder than words. I'm not perfect. Neither are you. But I do know one thing, if we allow ourselves to be molded by God he will make us into his perfect image. I'll talk to you when I get home tonight.

Love, Antonia

I knew that writing this letter would start me on the right path to communicating with my husband. I had done things a little different this time. I went and I got on my knees and spoke with my heavenly father to ask him what would be the best way to do things. I did not yell to God or tell him what I wanted him to do. I simply went to God and said, *"Lord, how do you want me to handle this?" "Allow me to see things how you see it, please give me the revelation and knowledge to understand how to talk to your child." "Please let me see him through your eyes so I can see what you see." "And I ask that you would give me the love necessary so that I could love my husband the way you love him Lord."* From then on my prayers started to be a little different.

God started to reveal to me that I needed to see things from a spiritual eye sight. And the only way that I was going to be able to do that was by really getting deep into God's word. So, I started picking up the Bible and doing devotions. I only really read the Bible when I went to church, but let me tell you something, we need to pick up the Bible every day and do devotions. How else is God going to communicate with us? How else can the Holy Spirit help us in our time of need? I needed to start building up my prayer life by being in constant prayer. Now, I am not saying that everything that was happening to me just ceased. No, that is not what I am saying at all. Everything was still the same, but this time around God was showing me how to handle things differently so that I could get through it. Because everything I dealt with, I dealt with in the flesh. Once I started dealing with it spiritually it no longer was my battle but the Lords.

"He said: "Listen, King Jehoshaphat and all who live in Judah and Jerusalem! This is what the LORD says to you: "Do not be afraid or discouraged because of this vast army. For the battle is not yours, but God's."
(2 Chronicles 20:15, NIV)

As I started to understand what that meant, my prayers became more purposeful. I was now praying to God that my husband would be able to know his worth and his value. My husband constantly was down on himself. He was always dwelling about his past and his failures. There were many times he would even say that he did not know why he was born.

The only way I could see my husband becoming the man I wanted him to be or being the husband I expected him to be was by seeing him through God's eyes. So as I started to pray diligently for my husband, and seek God's grace and mercy for my husband's life. God started to reveal himself to me and show me my husband in the future. God started to show me that my husband in the future would be a man of valor, he would be a provider, and that he would find himself loving himself.

I noticed that it didn't feel like there was love in my marriage because he was not lovable. Intimately, he wanted to be lovable, but not in the typical sense of lovable. How can my husband love me if he doesn't love himself? So I started praying for that love to come for my husband from God because once he loved himself, then he could love on other people. As much as I wanted this to take place quickly I knew everything would be according to God's timing.

As I started to truly hold on to God's promises, it was just a matter of time when I could see some results. This did not happen overnight because we all have to go through the valley. The lilies are there in the valley guiding us as we go through the valley. God's presence is there regardless of what we are dealing with. We just really need to know how to identify it. The more I prayed for my husband, the more peace and comfort came onto my spiritual being. And with time, little by little, I started to see peace also in my husband. It was baby steps, but a good start.

His tantrum and yelling was not as intense, and he was still doing the verbal abuse but with a different tone. It was just a new learning experience for both of us to see what God was really doing. Remember earlier when I said that I only came into the marriage with a cosmetic bag. Well the reality is that I too had baggage because when you have make up in your bag and you put it on your face. The makeup itself covers things up like spots, or blemishes, hides wrinkles, dark circles, puts a new face on you to make you look pretty or different. The makeup hides all those imperfections. I had issues as well. I started to understand that I too needed to change according to God's ways.

At the same time I stopped thinking negatively about my husband. I started thinking positively about him. I was no longer calling him a *"dead beat"* in my mind. I was now claiming in the name of Jesus that my husband was going to become a different man in the sight of God. That he was going to strive in life; and that God was going to heal him from all those hurts he had inside. I would pray that my husband was going to fulfill his purpose in life according to God's plan. That he would rightfully take his place as a husband and a provider. That he would release his negative thoughts as well and start thinking and speaking positive. I really started to believe this was going to happen. And I knew that I was going to see a new fruit in my husband. See the fruits of the spirit are very important. You can call yourself a Christian but if you don't operate in any of the fruits, you can consider yourself a fruitless person.

"But the fruit of the Spirit is love, joy, peace, kindness, goodness, faithfulness, gentleness, and self control." (Galatians 5:22-23, NIV)

That evening, when my husband arrived we had dinner and I started to talk to him about how I felt. I explained to him that I had given up my entire world, my acting, my friends, my lifestyle, etc. And that I had found myself uncertain about what I was doing, unhappy, etc. That I lost who I was as a person and that I needed to find myself again. I told him that I wanted to lose a lot of weight. I wanted to get back into acting and start auditioning again. *"My personality is very artsy and I want to continue to be creative."* I told him. I also asked him what did he want to do for himself and he mentioned to me that he no longer had dreams, that his dreams were dead. So I started to explain to him that God had shown me what he will look like in the future, but that I did not know how the journey was going to be in getting there.

It was a good start in communication. At least I got some things off my chest. And let me tell you; it felt really good to say those things. I felt like a monkey jumped off my back. I still had some guerrillas on my back but to have gotten one or two monkeys off, was a good start. I then assured my husband that I really wanted things to work out with us. I told him that I knew it was hard adjusting to a new place. However, I explained to him that we could get through this together. I also told him about some plans that we could work out together only if he was willing to do them. I remember Sassy even came over by us because there was actually a peaceful moment.

That night, I slept well. There was no need for my husband to wake me up in the middle of the night like he normally did because of my snoring due to my weight gain. It was peaceful and we both slept straight through till morning.

"Come to me, all you who are weary and burdened, and I will give you rest. Take my yoke upon you and learn from me, for I am gentle and humble in heart, and you will find rest for your souls. For my yoke is easy and my burden is light." (Matthew 11:28-30, NIV)

The next day when I woke up, I made breakfast and felt as though I could look forward to a future full of hope. I was relieved that I was really able to have the conversation with my husband the night before. As we ate, I was smiling because I thought to myself, yes, this is good, back on track, things will work out, it was a bump in the road but now we are good.

Then all of sudden, my husband blurted out that he didn't appreciate the fact about what I wrote in the letter. That he was actually insulted. All I could do was keep smiling and chew on my food. I swallowed and thought to myself, this was too good to be true, here we go again. Then I remember I got up from my chair and went into the kitchen to put my dish in the sink. My husband, blurted out, *"Don't walk away from me when I am talking to you."* I started to wash the dishes as he continued to insult me with his words about what he didn't like about me.

I took the dish rag dried my hands, went upstairs to my bedroom, got my handbag and I walked out the house. I got in my car and starting driving down the road as tears started flowing down my face. All I could say was *"Why Lord why?"*

TO BE CONTINUED

TODAY'S REFLECTION

When I think about the moment God spoke to me about writing this book. I paused for a moment and I said to God. *"You want me to write about my marriage?" "Ah, that's the last thing I want to write about."* However, I knew that if that was what the Lord was calling me to do now in this season of my life, then I was going to be obedient.

I remember asking God; *"Where do I start?"* And he said *"From the Beginning"*. Oh, I see, from the beginning, well that was going to take me way back. Back to when my husband and I met. I sat at my computer and I said to God, *"If I start from the beginning, God, I ask that you help me write this according to how you want it to be."* I started writing, and all of a sudden I came to a halt. I knew that in order for me to write accurately all the details, I needed to get my journals from New Jersey.

So I called up my husband and shared with him that God wanted me to write a book. Then I asked him if he could go into a cabinet where I had all my journals and if he could send them to me. He had no idea I had all those journals; especially the diary. I asked him not to read any of it but to just overnight them.

TODAY'S REFLECTION

When I received my journals and my diary, I started to read some of it and then I stopped. I specifically stopped because I was going down memory lane. And as far as I was concerned, God had delivered me from that past time. He had healed those wounds and brought me to a place of serenity. So, I asked God that before I would go any further to help me not be affected by what I was going to read, and to help me see it from a different perspective. I also said to God that I wanted this book to bless people. That the story I was going to share would help someone else. My past experience would be used to give insight to someone else in a similar situation or circumstance. And mostly that God would be glorified! So I started to read, and continued to write.

As I was reading, I said WOW. I really said those things, felt that way, and most of all got through it with God's Grace. I have learned so much since then. And I can proudly say that had it not been for that experience, I would not be the standing strong woman in Christ that I am today. God has been so good to me. And my relationship with my heavenly father continues to grow every day, as well with my husband. By the time this book is published, my husband and I will be married 17 years.

TODAY'S REFLECTION

So much has happened in my marriage that I wake up every day now saying, thank you God for everything.

I look back at my first two years of marriage and as I see myself in my 30's; I sure was ambitious. Everything I was trying to achieve was based on what I knew then. Today I know that life needs to be lived one day at a time. Whether in the good or bad times, I know that God is always by my side. So now in the present, when I encounter difficulties, or downfalls of any type, I just smile and say *"God I know you are in control."* I truly believe that and always will believe that, matter of fact, I just don't believe it; I live it. I live knowing that God is in control all the time!

I was 35 years old and so happy!

MESSAGE TO THE READER

I am excited to share *The Confessions Series* with you and I look forward to bringing the additional books that will tell the entire story *Confessions of a Christian Woman: A Journey in Marriage.*

For those of you who are reading this book and may be experiencing in your life a situation or circumstance with your boyfriend, husband, or significant other, I want to let you know that there is hope at the end of the tunnel. Even in our greatest time of despair, God is looking over us, whether we want to believe it or not. For me, my journey in marriage has at times been depressing, heart breaking, and most of all loveless. But I knew that as long as I pressed into my heavenly father and Jesus Christ for help with the guidance of the Holy Spirit, I would receive healing in my heart, my mind, my spirit, and my soul.

I am a Christian who believes that Jesus Christ died on the cross for my sins. That I am a new creation in Christ and that the relationship I have with him grows every day. I pray every day to Jesus Christ, God, and ask the Holy Spirit for guidance in my life. I received the baptism of the Holy Spirit back in the year 2001 after receiving Jesus

MESSAGE TO THE READER

Christ as my Lord and Savior in the year 2000. I was formally baptized by water (in the Ocean) in New York. That day for me became a new way of life. I instantly knew that something new had sparked inside of me, I couldn't explain it at the time, but I knew that I had Joy in me. That God had given me peace, comfort and most of all that he was preparing me for a new life with him.

I grew up Catholic and went to church on occasions, rarely read the Bible, and didn't really know anything about having a personal relationship with Jesus Christ.

In my life right now, I have a deeper relationship with God more than ever because I have received salvation from his son, Jesus Christ. As well I have learned and I know how to tap into the resource of the Holy Spirit to help me in my time of trouble. Every day I ask God for wisdom, knowledge and discernment for my life. So that I can hear his voice and I can make the proper choices. As I continue my Christian walk with Jesus Christ, I learn something new every day. It is one of the journeys in my life from the many journeys I have, and it is a beautiful journey.

I don't know where you stand right now, with believing or not believing in God, Jesus Christ, or the Holy Spirit. As a matter of

MESSAGE TO THE READER

fact, I don't even know if you are religious at all or even an atheist. Wherever you stand right now with your belief system, after reading this book, I pray to God that you have been blessed by the story I shared with you. Because no matter where we are in our lives right now, God wants to meet us and get to know us, and we should get to know him. The best way to get to know God is through his son, Jesus Christ.

The Bible depicts very clearly why God sent his beloved son, Jesus Christ to this earth many years ago, and the purpose he fulfilled when he was here in the flesh. If you are interested to know more about God, Jesus Christ, or the Holy Spirit, I recommend you get a Bible and start reading it. It can be acquired in a book store or online for free. There are many apps you can download on your phone or computer.

Many people ask me why am I still with my husband after everything I have been through in my marriage. I tell them that what I have endured in my marriage has actually been a blessing from God. I understand that very clearly today more than ever.

You as the reader may not understand my reason why I am still with my husband. As you continue to read the books I write, you

MESSAGE TO THE READER

eventually will understand. My question to you is; why are you still with your boyfriend, husband, or significant other? Do you right now want to walk away from that relationship? Are you frustrated with what is happening in the relationship? Do you find yourself in a situation or circumstance that you feel you have no control over? No matter how many questions I might ask you, there is a reason why you as a young lady or woman are still in the relationship.

As females, we have a natural sense about us where we want things to work out. We are looking for resolutions, resources, or even remedies to help us in the process of our relationships with males. There is hope that possibly things can change, that maybe we can change them, or one day they will change. The problem is that we do not get the results we want because we think that we are the ones that can bring forth all that change. Change can only take place with other people when there is change first within ourselves. Think about that for a minute. If you are a male reading this book, the same applies to you. See, we think that only females go through relationship problems; that it only occurs on their side and not the male side. Not true, there are many males who are in relationships just like the one I shared in this book.

Either way, all I can say to everyone is, God is good all the time and he can help you in your time of trouble. I know, because he helped me. God helped me change my thinking process, as well helped me understand how to deal with my husband in my marriage. As I continued to build my relationship with God he helped me understand how to build my relationship with my husband.

If he did it for me, he can do it for you. Are you ready for a change?

SIMPLE PRAYER

Dear God,

I know it's been a while since I have said hello to you. So today, I say hello and surrender my life into your hands. I find myself in a place right now where I am not happy. I need a drastic change in my life. I call on you to help me at this time. I want to surrender it all to you. I know that I can start by being on the right track with you God. Please show me the way so that I can do the right thing in your eyes. I need you in this situation or circumstance. You are the true God who can help me in my time of trouble. I pray for an opportunity to give my life to you and to receive Jesus Christ as my Lord and Savior.

(Now you can fill in the blank of some of the special requests you need from God)

_____

_____

_____

SIMPLE PRAYER

Continue writing your requests here

ABOUT THE AUTHOR

Antonia Roman is a Puerto Rican Native New Yorker. She was born in Brooklyn and raised in Long Island, NY. She started her career as an Actress in Musical Theater doing local and regional theater productions. In her early twenties she entered the Music Industry, first with a local Spanish band as a background singer and dancer. Then she moved on to doing backup vocals for performing R&B/Rap Artists. In her late twenties, Antonia attended Queens College where she acquired two Bachelor Degrees in Drama, Theater & Dance and Media Studies. After College, with the help of a friend, she transitioned to the Film/TV industry where she started out as a Production Assistant doing promo commercials for television. As time went by, she decided that she wanted to be in front and behind the camera. Antonia eventually started producing and directing projects. She also assisted in her local church in directing some of their theater productions. In 2014, Antonia started her production company, That's So Funny Entertainment. Her company brings creative ideas to life through Film, TV, and Theater productions.

ABOUT THE AUTHOR

Here I am on the Set of "Hollywood Tale"

Here I am on the Set of "Boricua in the House", with Actresses Katherine Damigos and Rosemary Lynne (Photo Credit: Burlington County Times)

Made in the USA
Middletown, DE
01 August 2019